MARK McGWIRE

RICHARD J. BRENNER

AN EAST END PUBLISHING BOOK

Mark McGwire became the greatest single-season home run hitter in major-league history by banging out 70 Big Flys during the 1998 season. Big Mac simply *shattered* the record of 61 homers that Roger Maris had set in 1961, hitting home runs faster and farther than any other player ever has.

"I've never seen anybody in all my years of watching baseball that absolutely crushed the ball as much as he does," said Hall of Famer Ted Williams, who became the last player to hit .400 when he racked up a .406 average for the Boston Red Sox in 1941. "I think people go to the ballpark to see if he's going to hit one over the moon."

Mark began hitting home runs as an eight-year-old, driving a ball over the right-field fence in his very first at bat for his Claremont (California) Little League team.

By the time he was ten, Mark had set the Claremont Little League record by hammering 13 homers, prompting an old-time baseball fan to offer a prediction to Mark's dad: "This kid, he's something. He's going to light up the world."

Mark continued his slugging at Damien High School, but he drew even more attention as a strong-armed pitcher who could throw heat at 90 miles per hour.

"He was born with talent," explained Tom Carroll, who coached Mark at Damien. "But he also worked hard, and that's what set him apart. Everyone has talents. Mark did something with his."

It was his pitching ability that won Mark a scholarship to the University of Southern California, but it didn't take long for USC coach Rod Dedeaux to decide that Big Mac was an even better hitting prospect.

"You could see the balls jumping off his bat every day at practice," said Dedeaux. "You didn't have to see a game to realize he had to play every day. When you saw him hit the ball nine miles, that was enough."

Mac went on to break the USC single-season home run record twice, hitting 19 in his sophomore year and a whopping 32 as a junior.

The Oakland Athletics were sold, selecting him in the first round of the 1984 amateur draft. And Mark rewarded the team's judgment, rising rapidly through the A's minor-league system, before breaking into the majors in a huge way by rapping a rookie-record 49 home runs.

Mac actually passed up a chance to try for 50 on the last day of the 1987 season, deciding instead to be present for the birth of his son, Matthew.

"It wasn't a tough decision," said Mac, who was a unanimous choice as the American League Rookie of the Year. "I'll never have another chance to have a first child, but I will have another chance to hit fifty home runs."

Although Mark didn't come close to hitting 50 homers during any of the next three seasons, he was a vital cog in an A's machine that won a trio of pennants and the 1989 World Series. In 1991, though, Mark's career suddenly headed south: His batting average sank to .201 and his home run total dove to 22.

"I was in a deep hole, and I didn't think I could climb out," said Mac, who thought seriously about quitting baseball.

But Mark did find the strength to come back and bang out 42 Big Macs in 1992. And while injuries sidelined him for most of the following two seasons, he resumed his hitting surge in 1995 and again in 1996, when he drilled 52 dingers. After he hit number 50, Mark retrieved the ball for his son. "You were my fiftieth homer in 1987," he told Matthew, "and this is my fiftieth homer now."

Mark continued his home run rampage in 1997, rapping a total of fifty-eight, 34 for the A's and 24 for the St. Louis Cardinals, who had obtained Mark in a July 31 trade.

Mark had joined the legendary Babe Ruth as the only other player to swat 50 homers in consecutive seasons, and Seattle Mariners outfielder Ken Griffey, Jr., had gone yard 56 times in 1997. So fans around the country were really looking forward to the 1998 season, wondering whether Big Mac or Junior might mount a challenge to the home run record that Maris had set 37 years earlier.

Mac stoked the excitement among fans and players at the beginning of the season by cracking king-sized home runs at a furious pace. "It was lucky that ball crashed into the scoreboard," joked Cleveland catcher Sandy Alomar after one of Mac's boomers. "Or else it goes around the world and hits me in the back of the head."

By the time play paused for the All-Star Game in early July, Mark had already bagged 37 Big Flys, putting him two up on Griffey and four ahead of Sammy Sosa, the Chicago Cubs right fielder who would dog Mac's pace for the remainder of the season.

Suddenly, Mac Mania was sweeping the country, as thousands of fans started showing up two hours before game time simply to watch Mark send balls soaring to faraway places during batting practice. Pitchers were booed in their home stadiums just for throwing a ball out of the strike zone to Mark, as the home run race added a country carnival atmosphere to the 1998 baseball season.

After Mark hit number 50 in the first game of a doubleheader against the New York Mets, the tension of the chase, which was magnified by the constant pressure of a huge media horde, seemed to ease for him.

"I've got my second wind," declared Mark, who proceeded to bash ten homers in 15 days, becoming the third player after Ruth and Maris to hit 60 in a season.

Two days later, Mac passed Ruth and tied Maris when he nailed number 61 in the first game of a two-game set against the Chicago Cubs. And the following night he wrote his name into the record book and electrified Busch Stadium when he lined his shortest homer of the season just over the left-field wall.

After the new home run king crossed home plate, he scooped up Matthew, saluted his parents, and then jumped into the stands to hug the children of Roger Maris and honor the accomplishment of their father.

Sosa, who wound up his own remarkable season with 66 dingers, came in from right field to hug Mark and tell him, "Don't go so fast. Wait for me."

But Mark kept right on going through his last swing of 1998, when he drilled the 70th home run of his spectacular season.

"I can't believe I did it," said Mark. "Can you? It's absolutely amazing. I'm proud of what I've been doing with Sammy Sosa. It's been a tremendous ride for him and for me. I'm in awe of myself right now."

If you enjoyed this book, you might want to order some of our other exciting titles written by Richard J. Brenner, the best-selling sportswriter in America.

Title   Qty.

BASEBALL SUPERSTARS ALBUM 1999. Includes 16 full-color pages of the game's top players, plus career stats. 48 pages. ($4.50/$6.50 Can.)   _____

BASKETBALL SUPERSTARS ALBUM 1999. Includes 16 full-color pages of the game's top players, plus career stats. 48 pages. ($4.50/$6.50 Can.)   _____

FOOTBALL SUPERSTARS ALBUM 1998. Includes 16 full-color pages of the game's top players, plus career stats. 48 pages. ($4.50/$6.50 Can.)   _____

MARK McGWIRE. An easy-to-read, photo-filled biography especially for young readers. 32 pages. ($4.50/$6.50 Can.)   _____

SAMMY SOSA. An easy-to-read, photo-filled biography especially for young readers. 32 pages. ($4.50/$6.50 Can.)   _____

MICHAEL JORDAN. An easy-to-read, photo-filled biography especially for young readers. 32 pages. ($3.95/$5.95 Can.)   _____

KOBE BRYANT. An easy-to-read, photo-filled biography especially for young readers. 32 pages. ($3.95/$5.95 Can.)   _____

GRANT HILL. An easy-to-read, photo-filled biography especially for young readers. 32 pages. ($3.50/$4.50 Can.)   _____

SHAQUILLE O'NEAL. An easy-to-read, photo-filled biography especially for young readers. 32 pages. ($3.25/$4.50 Can.)   _____

WAYNE GRETZKY. An easy-to-read, photo-filled biography especially for young readers. 32 pages. ($3.25/$4.50 Can.)   _____

Total number of books ordered.   _____

Postage and handling ($1.50 per book, up to a maximum of $7.50. $1.75, up to a maximum of $8.75 in Canada.)   _____

TOTAL PAYMENT ENCLOSED (Payment must accompany all orders. All payments must be in U.S. dollars.)   _____

SEND PAYMENT TO: EAST END PUBLISHING, 54 ALEXANDER DR., SYOSSET, NY 11791
Discounts are available for orders of 25 or more books. For details, write or call (516) 364-6383.

Photo Credits: The photo on the front and back covers was taken by **Stephen Dunn** and was supplied by ALLSPORT USA. The first three photos in the book were taken by **Tony Inzerillo**. The photos on pages 6, 9, 12, and 21 were taken by **Michael Zito**, **Rob Tringali, Jr.** (2), and **Steve Woltman** and were supplied by SPORTSCHROME. The photos on pages 15, 18, and 24 were taken by **Jonathan Daniel**. The last three photos were taken by **Jed Jacobsohn** (2) and **Elsa Hasch** and were supplied by ALLSPORT USA.

ISBN: 0-943403-48-0

AUTHOR'S NOTE: Mark McGwire has shown that beyond loving his own son, he is interested in all children by contributing a million dollars a year to the Mark McGwire Foundation, which provides help to abused children. "I would rather be associated with something I'm doing for my foundation than for anything I've done as a baseball player," said Mac, who has also shown true love for Matthew by maintaining a positive relationship with Matthew's mother, Kathy, Mark's former wife.